M. C Tyndall

Lays and Lyrics of England and Various Verses

M. C Tyndall

Lays and Lyrics of England and Various Verses

ISBN/EAN: 9783744775304

Printed in Europe, USA, Canada, Australia, Japan

Cover: Foto ©Thomas Meinert / pixelio.de

LAYS AND LYRICS OF ENGLAND

And Verses Various

BY

M. C. TYNDALL

J. BAKER & SON, CLIFTON

AND

25 PATERNOSTER SQUARE, LONDON

1898

AUTHOR'S NOTE

IT should be mentioned that six of the poems in this volume were published some years ago in a book entitled *Rhymes, Real and Romantic*, which is now out of print, and having been frequently asked for, they are reproduced here, and will be found in the following order:—

"The Wreck of the *Birkenhead*."
"In a Garden."
"Indian Summer."
"The Lost Churchyard."
"The Viking's Galley," and
"Elizabeth's Garden at Heidelberg."

CONTENTS

OF ROYAL ENGLAND

IN RURAL ENGLAND

CONTENTS

VERSES VARIOUS

CONTENTS

OF THE DAYS OF OLD—*BALLADS*

CONTENTS

IN THE COURTS OF THE TEMPLE

OF ROYAL ENGLAND

GOD'S GIFT TO ENGLAND

Jubilee Hymn

Tune—"St. Albans" (Haydn).

GLORY and thanksgiving
Be to God on high,
For the Queen He gave us
In the time gone by.
England's sons and daughters,
Here on English sod,
Praise for countless mercies
Render unto God;

For the stainless record
Sixty years have seen,
For the gift He gave us
In our gracious Queen!

England's sons and daughters
Come to keep the feast:
North and South and Westward,
And the restless East.

All her boundless Empire,
  Land and isle and sea,
Come their Queen to honour
  At her Jubilee!

    Glory and thanksgiving
      Be to God on high,
    For the Queen He gave us
      Sixty years gone by

Sixty years of Progress,
  Honour, freedom, fame,
Evermore extending
  England's ancient name.
Justice, truth, and mercy,
  Mark her sway benign,
Reigning well and wisely
  Longest of her line!

    Well may England's people,
      In exultant words,
    For the Queen He gave them
      Praise the Lord of Lords!

Praise Him for the blessings
  Righteous acts have wrought,
Christian work increasing,
  Powers of Evil fought;

Poor, and sick and sinful,
  Succoured, taught, and fed;
Deeds of mercy offered
  Unto Christ the Head.

    And our Queen stands foremost
      In all righteous ways,
    So for these His mercies
      Be to God the praise.

Praise for gifts unnumbered
  In this longest reign,
Wonders yet unfolding,
  That the years attain.
Manifold inventions,
  Sound, and steam, and light,
Enterprise exploring
  Field, and flood, and height.

    Unto God be glory
      Now and evermore,
    From all hearts in England
      Loyal as of yore!

Rise up, then, ye people!
  Every rank and creed,
All her loyal subjects
  Give our Queen God speed!

Pray that God may bless her,
  Guard her through all strife,
And at last may crown her
  With Eternal Life.

    Glory to the Father,
      Glory to the Son,
    And the Holy Spirit
      Ever Three in One!

"READY"

Suggested by the picture of a Lion on guard in *Daily Graphic* for January 11, 1896, the time of the war scare.

THE Nations watched Britannia with furtive
eyes of hate,
As calm she sat, and silent, above her narrow
strait;
They deemed her sunk in slumber, absorbed in
greed of gold;
They thought the Lion by her had grown effete
and old.

They marked the gathering war-clouds with ill-
disguised content:
"She stands alone, and friendless, and will not
dare resent!"
And thus the Nations muttered, till one rose in
his place
To hurl with reckless challenge an insult in her
face.

* * * * *

Who said Britannia slumbered? Who deemed her pride gone by?
Lo! every man in England has thrown them back the lie!
A sound thrilled through the Island, a growl the stillness brake,
The Nations wondered awestruck, the Lion is awake!

From seaboard unto seaboard, from Portsmouth to the Nore,
From Plymouth Sound to Spithead, all round the Southern shore,
In squadron after squadron, full armed from keel to peak,
The great war-vessels muster along the silver streak.

And o'er the dim horizon, from lands beyond the sea,
Her vast Colonial Empire, where British hearts beat free;
From North, South, East, and Westward, by ties of blood held dear,
Her children's loyal voices give their great Mother cheer.

Britannia rouses slowly, her patience suffers long,
But her wrath, once kindled, blazes before the
sense of wrong;
The spirit of their fathers her sons inherit yet,
And the Lion once awakened, he doth not soon
forget!

And thus before the Nations Britannia stands
and waits,
Her royal beast beside her to guard the narrow
straits;
"God and St. George for England!" the watch-
word of her might:
Heaven give us peace with honour, and God defend the right!

"BROTHER TO BROTHER SPAKE."*

ACROSS the great Atlantic with trumpet tongue there came
Brave words as bravely spoken, that flash as beacon flame;
Columbia's son for England, the threatened tension breaks,
Where Senators had blundered, brother to brother speaks!

"I see," he said, "the Nations with sullen scowl and sneer,
With hostile front to England, draw nearer, and more near;
All Europe linked together by bonds of envious hate,
In half ashamed Alliance, against the Island state.

* Speech by Senator Walcott (at Washington), February, 1896.

"I mark how England's people rise at their
Country's call,
Their hand upon the sword-hilt, united one and
all,
How shoulder unto shoulder her sons unflinching
stand,
In steadfast silence waiting what Duty may de-
mand.

"I see her mighty war-ships, the proudest Fleet
at sea,
From Port to Port preparing for what the end
may be;
Army and Navy joining to guard their Island
throne,
England against all Nations, undaunted and
alone!

"And as I watch and marvel, there thrills within my breast
A sympathetic fervour that will not be supprest;
The bond of blood is mighty, our race and theirs
is one;
I thank my God, exulting, I too am England's
son!

"Nay! till just cause divides them, let our great
Nations stand,
America and England, with hand fast clasped in
hand;
One blood, one tongue, one kindred, for glory
and for peace,
And God forbid that ever, their harmony should
cease!"

BEFORE AND AFTER

August–October, 1588

Before

WHEN good Queen Bess was on the throne,
And England well could hold her own,
And guard her Island shore;
While her proud sons stood sword in hand,
The bulwark of their native land,
When Raleigh, Drake, and Grenville fought,
And each their Country's honour sought
In the brave days of yore:
One August day, ere sun was set,
All England's great sea-captains met
To stroll on Plymouth Hoe;
To play at bowls in contest keen,
Or pace along the level green,
In converse weighing o'er again
The threatened armaments of Spain;
Debate what England's force could yield
Of ships or men, to take the field
Against the Popish foe.

*   *   *   *   *

That August night a message sped,
Which tipped the hills with lurid red;
  Each hill its fellow hailed.
It roused the land from shore to shore,
From Milford Haven to the Nore;
From Dartmoor Tors to Cotswold hill,
And by the coast to Portland Bill,
  While wives and maidens paled.
And men their harness buckled on,
And watched the midnight skies which shone
  With beacon fires aflame.
Darkness and dawn found Plymouth street,
Astir with sound of hurrying feet,
  Athrong with knights of fame;
And ships were manned, and anchors weighed,
As the High Admiral's orders bade;
For grave the tidings of the night,—
How off the Scilly Isles in sight,
Beyond the ending of the land,
Like some vast cloud that ocean spanned,
  The Great Armada came!

After

Where is that great Armada now?
Sealed to the Saints by prayer and vow,
  Blessed by the Pope's own hand?
Where are the arms and treasure stored,

Those lofty Galleons safe aboard?
Where are the puissant Dons of Spain,
Their tonsured friars, their armoured train,
And where the countless hosts who went
Proudly from Spanish shores intent
  To conquer Britain's land?

Go ask of Howard, Hawkins, Drake,
And heroes sailing in their wake,
  Their country to defend.
Go ask each gallant ship and crew,
Who bravely England's ensign flew,
Who mocked defeat, and fought, or fell,
The Spaniard's arrogance to quell;
Aye! let these English warriors tell
  The great Armada's end!

Where are those mighty Galleons, say,
With all the wealth that in them lay,
  Proud Spain's rich argosies?
Go, sound the Goodwin's deadly shoal,
And where the North Sea waters roll;
Go, search the crags of Flamborough Head,
The swirl of Tarbat's billows dread,—
And where Atlantic currents spread
  Round wind-blown Hebrides!

Ask of the lonely Orkneys, then,
For Galleons lost and drownèd men,
For wreck and ruin, dark and deep,
Where fierce white-crested breakers sweep
  Beneath relentless skies.

* * * * *

Nay! ask the winds of God which brought
Aid to the patriot band who fought,
And crowned the victory they wrought;
Ask of the ocean and the air,
The Heaven-sent storm and tempest,—where
  The great Armada lies!

AT HOUGOUMONT*

May 27th, 1896

ROUND Hougoumont the sunshine falls
  From cloudless skies of May,
Upon its circling orchard walls,
  And grassy slopes to-day.

The same old walls, all seamed and scarred,
  Defaced by shot and shell,
Which eighty summers back had barred
  The French advance so well.

And where their fire was spent in vain
  Against an unseen foe,
The broken loopholes still remain
  That stern defence to show.

* It is recorded that, after Waterloo, the Duke said the fate of the battle had turned upon the closing of the North Gate at Hougoumont.

The old North gate stands wide to-day,
  A hard-fought barrier then,—
Upon whose fateful closing lay
  Full many lives of men.

And though no tombstone marks the spot
  Where sleep those nameless slain,
Their gallant stand is ne'er forgot,
  The battered walls remain!

The sweet air stirs the dancing leaves
  Of apple boughs o'erhead,
But never heart is left who grieves
  For those unnumbered dead.

They lie in ranks around the wall,
  Or friend or foe the same,
Beyond the sound of bugle call,
  Beyond the reach of fame.

A broken wall, an ancient gate
  (So slight life's agents are)
Become the instruments of Fate,
  The obstacles of War!

OUR British soldiers need no pen
To tell their gallant deeds to men,
Their valour in the fight.
From age to age their praises roll
From sea to sea, from pole to pole,
Till Time itself fills up the scroll
In everlasting light!

'Neath Spanish sun, in Russian snows,
'Mid India's hordes of dusky foes,
They fought, the bravest brave,
In storm and siege, through fire and flood,
On many a battlefield of blood,
Have Britain's sons as victors stood,
Or found a glorious grave!

But not alone they meet their doom
Where sabres flash, and batteries boom,
And gallant hearts beat high;

For ne'er 'mid all the noble dead
Is a purer light of glory shed,
Than on those who in the *Birkenhead*
Have shown how heroes die.

Dark fell the night on storm and wreck,
The raging breakers swept the deck,
The ship was sinking fast.
The boats are launched—but what are they,
Those waiting hundreds to convey?
The few must go—the many stay—
Ah! who will be the last?

It is the question—Die or live?
And no reply the soldiers give;
They silently fall in.
They know the doom'd ship must go down,
They know that those who stay must drown,
They dream not of the high renown
Their sacrifice shall win!

Unmoved they stand 'mid flying foam,
As in the barrack-yard at home,
In martial line arrayed.
Calmly the Colonel gave the word,
And silently the soldiers heard,
While from the ranks not one man stirred,
They stood as on parade.

And while the angry waves rose high,
Steadfast they waited there to die,
    And, in their ranks, went down.
There side by side in fathoms deep,
Until the last Great Day they sleep,—
But English hearts shall ever keep
    For them a hero's crown!

A FAREWELL TO THE COLOURS

TRAMP of troops in step advancing,
  Sharp the word rings out—" Right wheel ! "
Clank of arms, the sunlight glancing
    On the steel.

With their band to lead them, march they,
  All astir the cloistered street;
By the old Cathedral archway
    Drums are beat.

With the colours borne exalted,
  For the last time on before,
Till within the Precincts halted
    At the door.

Then, the white-robed clergy leading,
  Pass the escort—rank and file,
With the colours still preceding,
    Up the aisle.

March they on, nor pause, nor falter,
  With the colours of the Crown;
Till the Priest upon GOD'S Altar
    Lays them down.

Lays them down each war-worn colour,
  Crossways on the Altar there,
With their battle-roll of valour
      Blazoned fair.

There the flags first consecrated,
  Marred by war, and shot, and smirch,
Now once more are dedicated
      By the Church.

And to Heaven on high appealing,
  Voices rise, and prayers are said ;
All alike, in reverence kneeling,
      Bend the head.

Then the colours, carried slowly
  For the last time to their place,
In the transept's shadow holy
      Find a space.

Sounds the band in cadence solemn,
  Booming dirge-like, sad and slow,
Echoed back by arch and column
      As they go.

But with measured tread retreating,
  Many a gallant spirit fell,
When the brave old colours greeting
      In farewell!

"AND THE TOAST WAS DRUNK IN SILENCE"

THEY called for the health of "The Queen,
    God bless her!"
  And loyally cheered it with three times three;
Confusion they drank to each foreign aggressor
  Who dares call in question her sway of the sea.

Came the word—"Now, gentlemen, fill your
    glasses,
  'To the Old Battalion' the toast shall run";
And the cheers ring out, as the wine re-passes,
  What the "fighting Forties" have dared and
    done!"

A pause, till the Colonel once more has spoken:
  "There is one last toast I would give," he said,
"To be drunk in silence by word unbroken—
  'The immortal names of our honoured Dead.'"

The comrades who served with the war-worn
colours,
Who fought and who bled in the old Brigade,
And who now, set free from all earthly dolours,
Are waiting the call to their last parade.

Amid Afghan passes, or Russian trenches,
In the din of battle, and storm of shot,
With a British pluck that ne'er brags nor blenches,
Till the roll-call sounded, and they were not!

"To our Dead, whose fame is to us undying,"—
Rose up every man in a hush profound,
And in silence where there is no replying,
In a solemn silence the Toast went round.

"THE WOODEN WALLS OF ENGLAND"

June, 1897

"THE wooden walls of England!" the bulwark of her shore,
Which made her Empire mighty in valiant days of yore,
Those memories undying that Time can ne'er efface,
Retake a living semblance this Jubilee of grace

In heyday of the season, with golden June aglow,
And life at highest tension, all movement, life, and show,
Along the great Queen's highway, through shining streets astir,
New wooden walls of England rise up to welcome her!

Before the royal palace, beside the shady park,
From street to street extending, as far as eye can mark;

And all along St. James's, and on towards the
Strand,
The way is all stockaded with scaffolding and
stand!

From Westminster to Southwark, Whitehall to
Temple Bar,
From Fleet Street to the Borough, rise paling,
plank, and spar,
Till where in solemn grandeur the vast cathedral
shows
Its majesty half shrouded, where wooden walls
enclose.

The wooden walls of England! In song so well
renowned,
Held loyal hearts and valiant, to sail the seas
around,
To bear the sons of England to distant lands unseen,
And now *their* children's children come back to
greet the Queen!

For still through England's Empire beat loyal
hearts and free,
Who fain their Queen would honour, her year of
Jubilee;

In countless throngs they muster, and thus it
well befalls
That England's mighty City stands fenced in
wooden walls!

THE ENSIGN OF ENGLAND

National Song

FOR CHILDREN'S VOICES. *Air*—"Bonnie Dundee"

WE are children of England! the land of the free,
With her Empire far reaching from sea unto sea,
From Canadian Dominion, Australia, Ceylon,
O'er all the vast countries the sun sets upon;
From the African deserts, to plains of Bengal,
There the Ensign of England floats over them all!

We are children of England! We all have a claim
In the glorious heroes who built up her fame!
Though we cannot fight battles, or govern our land,
Yet the youngest among us, himself may command,
Be true and God-fearing, obedient and brave,
While the Ensign of England doth over us wave.

We are children of England! Then let it be
seen,
That we honour our Country, our Church, and
our Queen!
That the proud name of England, we glory to
speak,
The friend of the friendless, the shield of the
weak!
Dear land of our fathers! Long, long may it be
That the Ensign of England floats fearless and
free!

THE CHURCH SCHOOLS OF ENGLAND

IN the old time England's glory in her National
Schools was nurst,
Where her children learnt, undoubting, that the
fear of God comes first;
Learnt to honour God's commandments—do the
right, nor count the loss,
By Baptismal grace anointed, as the soldiers of
the Cross!
So beneath the Church's guidance, year by year
they onward grew,
Men and women strong and steadfast, keeping
England's honour true.

Now, the stress and strain of living, pride of
learning, greed of gain,
Mars the simpler, truer teaching, deems it obsolete
and vain;
And there are in Christian England, schools, not
one, but more to-day,
Where, alas! God's little children are not even
taught to pray!

And the Church which fain would train them in
the godly ways of old,
Sees the Faith the fathers cherished, in their sons
grow faint and cold.

Shall it be that English children, in this so-called
age of light,
With the powers of Evil rampant, are unguarded
in the fight?
Careless of the God who made them, ignorant of
Creed, or prayer,—
Shall our ancient Church forsake them, these
young souls beneath her care?
Nay! Let loyal hearts, uniting, hold the Faith
the saints adored,
Training England's sons and daughters in the
service of the Lord!

IN RURAL ENGLAND

IN A GARDEN

A FAIR old Garden, still and silent lying
In the calm sunlight of October days,
With just a breath of Autumn chillness sighing
Amid those mellow rays.

A dim blue haze broods o'er the distant meadows,
While sunshine on the ancient city falls,
Shining o'er spire and roof, or gabled shadows
Of ivy-covered walls.

On sloping lawns, the late dews, gleaming brightly,
Leave in the shade white webs of gossamer,
Where yellow leaves float down to earth so lightly
As scarce those threads to stir.

Tall hollyhocks bend languid in the border,
Where marigolds and stocks still linger on;
But bronze for green, and tangled stems for order,
Tell Summer days are gone.

Ilex, arbutus, hollies tall, are framing
  In sombre green the fires October lights;
In red and gold, the chestnut fans out-flaming
    Against the mist-crowned heights.

And, ranged along the terrace-walk, great aloes
  Year after year their destiny await;
That crownèd mystery of flower that hallows
    The irony of Fate.

For since that Garden first in order blended,
  More than a hundred years have come and gone;
And still majestic, 'mid green lawns extended,
    The old house stands alone.

And there our dearest, holiest memories meet us,
  From cloudless childhood unto later years;
And all the happy past comes back to greet us,
    Half sunlight and half tears.

Ah, dear old Garden! Tender thoughts surround thee,
  And murmur low among the murmuring trees—
Life-shadows that the years have twined around thee
    Of other days than these.

—THE FORT, *October*, 1882.

INDIAN SUMMER

A Recollection of Clevedon, 1881

THE aftermath of Summer, ere she flies
Swift-footed to the South, where snows are not,
A dream revived of glowing August skies
Which well-nigh are forgot.

What though September's torch in blazing light
Has kindled into flame the woodland ways?
The sunny scene, in Summer's colours dight,
Her counterfeit displays.

Still is the noontide air with sun aglow,
Nor felt as yet the twilight's subtle chill;
The only sound, ripe leaves descending slow,
Or Robin's tuneful trill.

Thy dreams of days departed, that enlace
With this bright Indian Summer's tranquil spell,
Fit well the aspect of this ancient place,
Where bygone memories dwell.

The old Court standing gabled, ivy-clad,
  Irregular, in stately length appears,
So old that ere the Tudor came it had
    A history of years.

Above, in tiers along the steep hillside,
  That ilex, and arbutus branches shade,
With warm brick walls that bowery creepers hide,
    Green terraces are laid.

And in their sunny shelter myrtles grow,
  Late, lingering roses faintly fragrant yet;
While marigolds with tints of Autumn glow,
    And tall green mignonette.

And o'er the wall, in wreaths of flaming red,
  Their scarlet sway Virginia creepers hold;
And down the hill, the beech and chestnut spread
    Their boughs of green and gold.

While far away lie tracts of mead and lea,
  And dim blue hills, that stretch in broken line
To where the sunlight on the Severn sea
    Spreads wide in silver shine.

Fair Indian Summer! days that fleet too fast,
  The year's calm aftermath ere hushed in sleep,
How many holy memories of the past
    Thy tranquil pictures keep!

A SOMERSETSHIRE GARDEN

ABBOTS LEIGH

THE Garden blooms to greet again
  Fair Spring in robes of grace,
With lilac bowers, and golden chain,
  Which childhood's days retrace;
When first we knew dear hearts and true,
  That guard this happy place.

The May is white on briar and bush,
  The lawns are daisy spread,
The mowing grass grows long and lush,
  Where sorrel spikes show red.
And far on high, the Cuckoo's cry,
  Comes clearly overhead.

Before the Garden porch there glows
  A Garden fair to see,
Where green and fresh the prospect shows
  Of flower, and shrub, and tree,—
A well-known spot, where, ne'er forgot,
  Live memories dear to me.

The smooth-cut lawns slope down to where
  The terrace walk is made,
The old Larch tree spreads wide and fair,
  Its feathery green arcade,
Where many a gay, sweet Summer's day
  We sat beneath its shade.

Beside the terrace walk in line,
  Is set a border bright,
Sweet Nancies, Wallflowers, Columbine,
  And Lupins blue and white;
And down below, the Chestnuts show
  Their branches flower bedight.

Grass fields beyond the Garden are,
  With hedgerow Elms beside,
Rich miles of country reaching far
  Towards the Severn tide,
Whose waters shine, where in dim line
  The blue Welsh hills stretch wide.

The sun upon that Garden seems
  As if it ever shone,
And loved ones walk there in our dreams,
  Who now from earth have gone,
But as of old, in love's fast hold
  Their memory lives on.

And still, thank God, dear friends remain
  Who keep that garden green,
And give sweet welcome full and fain,
  As it hath ever been.
So Spring's bright reign paints o'er again
  That well remembered scene.

Sunday Evening in Spring

SOFT breath of Spring, fair gleams of May
upon the garden green,
Where lilac boughs are mingled with laburnum's
golden sheen;
And gay with flowers along the lawn, backed by
the tall elm trees,
A sweet old-fashioned border runs, the haunt of
murmuring bees.
And from the ancient town hard by, in rhythmic
cadence slow,
The chime of bells for Evensong, comes softly to
and fro.

And down the slopes the birches hang their
feathery catkin wreaths,
And yellow gorse upon the bank, a subtile fragrance breathes:
While in the border columbines, and polyanthus
show

With tulips gay, and asphodel, and wallflowers
all ablow.
And still from many a smoke-stained tower, borne
on the light spring air,
The Bristol bells are chiming out their call to
praise and prayer.

A Sunday calm seems brooding o'er the garden's
shady place,
The town's dull stir of busy life is hushed a little
space;
The shadows lengthen o'er the grass, the sunlight
falling low
Lights up the old house on the slope, where many
windows glow;
While mingled with the evening bells, in drowsy
monotone,
The echo of returning rooks upon the breeze is
blown.

The city and the distant hills, are bathed in even-
ing light,
For Bristol lifts her misty veil of smoke on
Sunday night,
Her spires and towers, and clustered masts of
ships along the quay

Shine out beyond the fresh Spring trees, a picture fair to see.
Ah! many a tale of years gone by, that old town garden tells,
But through them all a cadence runs,—the chime of Bristol bells!

IN THE WEST COUNTRY

FAIR are the blue May morning skies
When Earth is innocent and sweet,
Ere Summer's fervid suns arise
To stir Spring's pulses into heat.

Fair are the dim Welsh hills that bar
The view beyond the Severn's sheen,
And fair the broad marsh meadows are,
With hedgerow elms in tender green.

Those rich marsh meads where clover blows,
With bowery hedges stretching wide,
Where her snow wreath the white May throws
Along the green West Country side!

In yellow buttercups knee-deep
The soft-eyed cattle ruminate,
Where cuckoo flowers, and cowslips steep
The air with fragrance delicate.

Grey gabled homesteads landmarks make,
  Adown the backward path of Time,
Where rosy apple orchards break
  The vivid green of larch and pine.

Down in the West the live-long day,
  The thrush's song sounds shrill and clear,
The joyous Sun, the scent of May,
  Combine to greet the glad young year.

Oh, fair the season! fair the scene!
  When Spring hangs out her braveries,
For none can tell when woods are green,
  How sweet the fair West Country is!

THE LOST CHURCHYARD

BLUE the sky, and blue the sea-line—blue, unfathomable, vast—
Dazzling in its pure effulgence, sea and sky together cast;
Not a breath in air or ocean, wafts the cloudlets feather-white,
Or the sunlit ripples glancing, glinting into sparks of light.
Far away the white coast shimmers, mist-like off St. Alban's head,
And near by the cliffs of Portland, with their rocky boulders spread;
While the tower of Bow and Arrow, frowns above the little bay,
Where the lap of sleepy wavelets hardly stirs the fair June day.

Soft and deep the castle's shadow, falls across the mossy turf,
While the white-winged seagulls soaring, bring a memory of the surf,

Memory of the surf and storm-drifts, in far other days than these,
When the salt breeze blowing landwards bore the spray of angry seas.
—Now where beech woods nestle sea-blown, in that rocky gorge and bare,
Where no foot of man disturbing, breaks the summer stillness fair,—
There, below the rocky headland, and beside the quiet waves
Is a Churchyard all forsaken, with its long-forgotten graves!

And amid grey rocks and boulders, marred and weather-stained as they,
There the old Church lies in ruins, ev'n its outlines swept away.
Silent now the bell for Vespers, chiming o'er the summer seas,
And where solemn Mass was chanted, only sound the murmuring trees;
Where the sailors brought their offerings to the Island Church of yore,
Nought remains but crumbling fragments, and the green graves by the shore;
Where the nameless dead are resting, laid there in the long ago,
Who or what, those quiet sleepers, no man ever now shall know.

Ev'n their memory lost, forgotten, in the silent
Past gone by,
Yet—oh, wondrous thought and solemn!—every
name is known on high,
And it may be in the gloaming, or when falls
the still midnight,
That their spirits sometimes wander by those
graves below the height,
Where white clover clusters shyly, and the bents
grow tall and green,
'Mid the grey rocks in the sunshine, with the
bramble-wreaths between.
And beyond,—blue sky and sea-line, melting mist-
like far away,
By the shores of Portland Island radiant in the
fair June day!

THE HILL OF THE SEVEN BARROWS

THE salt breeze sweeps across the downs, the
rolling downs of close-cropped turf,
That lie along the Ridgeway road, within the
echo of the surf,
Steep slopes of green against the sky, and far
away the sea's long reach,
The silver sheen of Deadman's Bay, beyond the
distant Chesil Beach.

All still and lone lies Bincombe Down, beneath
blue Summer skies aglow,
Backed by the sea-blown woods of Came, with
Bincombe Village far below.
So still, save for the sheep bells' sound, the larks
that carol out of sight,
And hum of wandering bees that seek the breath
of thyme and clover white.

So still, and yet that peaceful height, above the
fields, above the sea,
Is haunted by a presence dread, that veils the
hills in mystery.
For there, set clear against the sky, by seven's
mystic number known,
In grass-grown mounds along the ridge are seven
ancient barrows shown.

The ancient graves where chiefs of fame were
laid to rest in mail and might,
To rest upon the green chalk downs, far from
the fury of the fight.
The spoils of war lie buried there, with shield
and spear on either hand,
And drinking horn, and treasure stored, to speed
them to the unknown Land.

We may not know the fight they fought, nor
count the number of the slain,
We may not know the hearts that broke for
those who ne'er came back again;
We muse of who and what they were, but Time
is dumb, and answers not,
The salt breeze brings no spell to break the
silence of that lonely spot.

Perchance when midnight gales arouse to tempest
all the dark West Bay,
Or when the Summer moonlight bathes the hills
in lustre as of day,
Perchance those ancient warriors stand in ghostly
phalanx face to face,
And clash of arms, and battle cries, sound dimly
o'er the haunted place.

Perchance! But with the dawn they pass, the
morning mist-wreaths fade and break,
The east grows rosy o'er the sea, the larks rise
up, the daisies wake:
The seven mounds on Bincombe Down catch the
first rays of morning light;
Those relics of the ancient Past—the seven barrows
on the height.

MY HOUSE OF DREAMS

ON the slope of the hills with the view before it,
Of the plain where the silver Severn gleams,
With the clustered roses and ivy o'er it,
It stands in the sunlight — "My house of dreams!"

There are Spanish chestnuts, great elms and beeches,
Their branches far spreading in chequered shade;
O'er the smooth-cut lawns with their long green reaches
Which slope to the edge of the woodland glade;

Of the wood that covers the hill's steep shoulder,
Where woodpigeons croodle, and thrushes sing,
Where the streamlet sparkles by mossy boulder,
And primroses carpet the path of Spring!

"My house of dreams!" with its carven gables,
Each lattice alight in the sun's last rays;
With its old walled gardens, and range of stables,
And the dark yew hedge where the sunflowers blaze!

Beyond the gate, is the road descending,
Through the village street to the lower ground,
By the ancient Church with its grey tower blending
In the soft green shade of the trees around.

And at evensong come the sweet bells chiming,
And the sound of the rooks as they linger late;
As the village people come slowly climbing
The wide Church steps to the old lych gate.

So fresh and so fragrant the glamour o'er me,
In the spell of the green West Country seems
The picture so vivid that shines before me;
And yet,—it is only a "House of Dreams!"

CLOVELLY

THERE is a haven far to find,
Beside a sapphire sea;
And, borne upon the Summer wind,
The scene comes back to me!

So fresh the trees, so green the sward,
The sea and sky so fair;
As if no Winter ever marred,
And June was always there!

In wooded gorge that cleaves the cliff
The clustered houses rise;
Their gables quaintly piled, as if
Thrown there in sportive guise.

They guard in odd, uneven line,
The stairway of the street,
Where rugged stones in steep incline
Echo the passing feet.

In sunny nooks, green garlands stray
With climbing roses bright;
Tall myrtles grow along the way,
By casements flower bedight.

Above the village in the shade,
Great oaks and beeches tower;
Green stretch of park and mossy glade
Befringed with fern and flower.

While down below,—anear, afar,
One plain of boundless blue,—
On to the distant harbour bar,
Beyond the cliffs in view.

The summer tide laps idly by,
Each ripple shining clear,
Where fishing-boats at anchor lie
Beside the little pier.

Such is the haven, calm and fair,
Mirrored in Ocean's breast,—
'Mid Summer sun, and balmy air
Down in the bowery West!

"WELCOME as the flowers in May!"
Goes the old-world greeting;
As the white thorn's scented spray,
As the wind-flowers of a day,
Freckled cowslips, "Keys of Spring,"
Purple orchis blossoming,
Sweets for her, my Sweeting!

Welcome! as the May-buds are,
So my winsome maid is!
As the faint, sweet primrose star,
"Five o'clocks" * that float afar,
Hedgerow violets softly blue,
When "Rogation flowers" † are few,
Spear-like lords and ladies!

* Dandelions gone to seed.
† Milkwort.

Welcome! welcome! gorse aglow,
Bids us kiss unchidden;
Blooms the heartsease for her now,
"Love in idleness,"* I trow.
Cuckoo flowers, and woodruff sweet,
And the wild thyme 'neath her feet,
Welcome her unbidden!

Welcome! Fairest flower is she,
Fresh as "water crazies!"†
Straight as sorrel on the lea,
Sweet as clover blossoms be.
So let May her welcome bring,
While "St. George's bells"‡ do ring
All my true love's praises!

* Pansies.
† Marsh Marigold.
‡ Wild Hyacinth.

IN SUMMER TIME

IN Summer time—the long blue day is sweet,
With hum of bees in honey-laden lime;
While gay birds echo from their green retreat
A joyous chant of roundelay and rhyme.
And fragrant breath of roses fills the air,
When June is June, and all the earth is fair
In Summer time.

In Summer time—the white moon-daisies star
Lush meadow grass which waits the glad year's prime,
Where sorrel spikes, and crimson clover are.
In bowery hedges, honeysuckles climb,
And yellow flags and meadow-sweet grow high
Beside the pool where lilies watch the sky,
In Summer time.

In Summer time—through perfumed garden gloom,
On warm, still nights, the silver moon sublime
Shines o'er pale stars of jessamine abloom;
And lovers linger till the midnight chime
In dream of bliss, all earthly care above,
For all the happy air breathes life and love,
In Summer time.

A SUMMER NIGHT

"A SUMMER night!" Hushed is the day's
unrest,
The toil and travail, and the fret of fight:
Calm is the great Earth mother's throbbing breast,
For healing sleep with her dim veil has dressed
The Summer night.
That veil mysterious, which since the light
Died in a sea of glory in the West,
Has wrapped in blessèd dark the Summer night.

"A Summer night!" Pale as some ghostly guest,
The clustering roses glimmer wan and white;
In odorous air syringa stands confessed,
And evening primrose lifts her transient crest.
Through all the night
Their gayer sisters sleep, for day bedight,—
And bird and breeze are hushed in slumb'rous
rest,—
So still, so sweet, the spell of Summer night!

"TALLY HO!"

"'TIS the sport of all sports! with a clear, wintry sky,
And the hoar frost enough just the furrows to dry;
With the wind from the South and the scent running high
  As we jog to the meet near or far.
Why, the whole country side is afoot and astir!
On wheels or on horseback, in fustian or fur,
On thoroughbred hunters, or screws from the town;
Young and old mixed together, some up and some down,
  At the meet they are all on a par!

There's the master, whose mount cost him hundreds of pounds,
With the farmer who's breaking a young one to hounds;

And the old sporting parson who halts on his
rounds,
And will wait—"just to see if they find!"
There's the boy fresh from school, and the girls
from the Hall,
In an eager assemblage, they wait one and all;
While the huntsman and whips with the hounds
lead the way
To a spinney near by, where the knowing ones
say,
There were foxes for time out of mind!

Now the horn tootles faintly—a whimper—a cry,
Down the side of the covert a whip gallops by,
And the field wait in silence, suspense waxing
high,
Till we hear ringing out—"Tally ho!"
"It's a find!" "No, it's not"—"Yes, it is!—
they're away!"
With the fox going straight as a die (well he
may!)
As the pack breaking covert lay hold of the scent,
And horses and men give excitement a vent
As away across country we go!

Not a cloud or a care on the spirit can lurk,
On a rattling good horse settling down to his
work,

Who the stiffest of fences was ne'er known to
        shirk;
  'Tis the sport of all sports, I contend,
When the ruck have tailed off, to be in the first
        flight,
With the pick of the field, and the hounds well
        in sight,
Sixty minutes with never a check going well,
And then just as the pace is beginning to tell,
  With a kill in the open to end!

Aye! even if when with the night coming down,
One is ten miles from home with a horse fairly
        blown,
In the wet and the cold, yet no drawback we
        own,
  If the sport has been good in the day!
Let the Socialists talk!—there's in England one
        place,
Where by merit alone, men are judged in the race;
For plebeian and peer in the hunting field meet,
At the good English sport that no other can
        beat—
  So "long life to fox-hunting," I say!

THE GREAT FROST OF 1890–91

The Thames at Blackfriars

A SPELL is on the river, a silence as of death,
A solitude surpassing, the Frost King's frozen breath;
No stir of life arising, no sound to break the gloom,
Save ice-floe grating weirdly, while dull fog-signals boom.

No sight of sail or shipping, the sluggish tide-waves stir,
Till where one lonely vessel lies moored at Westminster;
In ice her keel is frozen, her rigging edged in snow,
The ghost ship in a vision of Arctic frost and floe.

The Sun's red disk shows dimly through mist-
wreath and through murk,
Where ice-blocks piled together, 'neath dark bridge
arches lurk;
The starving sea-gulls hover, o'er Temple's frozen
stair,
And midday chimes strike muffled in chill and
darkened air.

From Westminster to Wapping, from Lambeth to
the Pool,
Along the banks at Southwark where icy currents
cool;
From Bermondsey to Blackfriars, down under
London Bridge,
From Charing Cross to Chelsea, the ice lies ridge
by ridge.

The mighty heart of London, its ceaseless stir of
men,
Its tireless toil and turmoil, what hushed it thus,
—and when?
The waterway of nations, the world's historic
stream;
The Great Frost holds it spell-bound, as phantom
of a dream!

January 10, 1891.

BY a river, by a river, in the dim dead days
 of old,
Through the waste low-lying marshes, and the
 reed beds green and gold,
Rowed the armoured Roman galleys, with the
 sweep of mighty oars,
Bearing Rome's all-conquering legions to the unknown Island shores.

By a river spreading havoc, with three hundred
 sails aloft,
Came fierce Danish hordes advancing, scattering
 terror once and oft;
There too, Saxon Edward building, holy fane at
 Westminster,
Died in peace, and left his country to the foemen
 threatening her.

By a river, by a river, in the zenith of his power,
At the conqueror's word commanding, rose the
bastions of the Tower,
And hard by where turbid currents rushed beneath its lofty ridge,
Where the gabled houses cluster, swept the span
of London Bridge.

By a river, far and farther, as the swift years
silent glide,
Spreads the giant City onward, East or West on
either side,
Palaces of prince or noble, with their water
gates below,
Ships athrong, with treasure laden, wait upon its
ebb and flow.

By a river, gilded barges bore the gay Court to
Whitehall,
Bravely decked, while song and music o'er the
placid waters call.
So, too, by the river darkly, when the nights
were long and late,
Many a mournful boatload passing, landed at the
Traitor's Gate.

By a river, pomp and pageant—battered hulk or
vessel proud,
Toil and triumph—trade and treasure, mingle in
a ceaseless crowd.
By a river, by a river, is proud England's flag
unfurled,
And this same all puissant river is the Highway
of the World!

WHITE WINGS

There is a Cornish legend that the white sea-birds are the spirits of drowned mariners.

OH! white wings that flash in the still Summer eve,
When the sea sinks to sleep in the lap of the day,
Or like phantoms appear where the white horses heave,
And lash their white manes into torrents of spray!

Are they ghosts of the drowned who lie thick in the sea,
Off the wild Cornish coast, and the lost Lyonesse?
Are they ghosts who their weird must eternally dree,
Swept along in the whirlpool of storm-wrack and stress?

'Mid the wash of the waves, and the wail of the wind,
Like a lost soul that strives for articulate speech;
'Mid the skirl of the stones that the surf leaves behind,
As it breaks in long roll on the pebble-strewn beach.

White wings! Are they ghosts of the years that are gone,
Where they hover and swoop in the trough of the sea?
Misty white as the foam the wave-summits upon,
Flashing swift as the blast when the tempest blows free?

Are they ghosts of the sea-kings who empire did keep
O'er the seas, in the gay gallant days that are dead?
Ghosts? Ah me! who shall measure the secrets asleep
Where the dim silent depths of the ocean are spread!

Oh! the sound of the sea, and the wash of the
waves,
Where the fierce breakers shudder, and cross-
currents surge,
And for ever and ever mourn over those graves
All unnamed, and unknown,—their monotonous
dirge!

THE SWAN SONG

SWANS! Like to snow wraiths for ever onward gliding,
Silently and softly as the phantoms of a dream;
Ah! could ye tell of the fairy secrets hiding
Down among the rushes where the silver ripples gleam!

Would ye could sing to us the song of the river,
Flowing in the shadow of the alders green and cool;
Or where in sunlight the circled shallows quiver,
And speckled trout are lurking in every glassy pool.

Swans! Did ye come where the yellow flags and sedges
Grow with crimson willow herb, and creamy meadowsweet?
Where brilliant dragonflies haunt the river's edges,
And the blue forget-me-nots, and water-lilies meet?

Say, did ye linger beneath the drooping beeches,
In the green reflection of their branches dipping low?
Or swim in the sunshine beyond the silent reaches
Where the purple kingfishers are flitting to and fro?

Ah! we may ask, but no voice comes back in greeting,
Slowly, ever silently those fair swan spirits glide;
Comes ne'er a whisper along the rushes fleeting,
None may know the hidden song a-drifting down the tide!

Yet o'er the river a murmur floateth sighing,
"Death it is alone that makes all earthly secrets clear."
So legends tell that it only is in dying,
Echoes of the swan's wild song come sadly o'er the mere!

1879.

A NOSEGAY

FLOATS down the years a memory sunlit, dim,
Calm with the peace of young, unquestioning days,
It shows the vision of a nosegay trim
And fair to childish gaze.

It shows an old town Church with whitewashed roof,
With singing gallery, and with high box-pews;
Where scattered worshippers without reproof
Might through long sermons snooze.

It shows the reverend preacher set aloft,
Black-gowned with theme monotonous, austere;
The rustle of the Churchyard trees sighs soft,
And chirp of sparrows near.

It shows the ancient clerk who giving out
With quavering drone, the psalm—"Come let us sing"—
Hears from the gallery in respondent shout
Stentorian voices ring.

Through dusty panes, the clear spring sunbeams
lie
Along the walls which marble tablets grace;
Along the royal hatchment set on high
And o'er the old clock face.

They shine upon the crimson curtained seat,
Where Warden's wands of office stand beside;
With lavish nosegays bunched in quaint conceit,
Decked out for Whitsuntide.

"A Nosegay!" Ah! were ever bunches seen
Like those old Whitsun posies of the past?
Where sprays of sweetbriar and of lads'-love
green,
A homely fragrance cast!

To old alms-women nodding in the aisle,
Those simple scents bring memories of past
days,
Of cottage gardens left a weary while,
And happy country ways.

There lilac, wallflowers, tulips find a place,
And even gaudy peonies are fixed;
With early pinks, and pansies quaint of face,
In bold confusion mixed.

Defiant of Ecclesiastic lore,
  That sleepy, sunlit memory from afar,
Yet a dear vision of the days of yore
  Those old Church nosegays are!

VERSES VARIOUS

NURSERY RHYMES

Up to Date

AH! child of the century! what shall we sing
to you?
The old songs and ditties no longer can thrill;
The death of Cock Robin no sorrow will bring
to you,
Nor the sad misadventures of Jack and his Jill.

With you, Nursery rhymes stand in humble
minority,
You scorn the refrain of each time-honoured
saw,
And regard as a case for the Poor-law authority,
The sleeping arrangements of Margery Daw!

You slight the three mice and their loss anato-
mical,
You care not how twinkles each little bright
star:
No wonder! you study the chart astronomical,
And say that "you know very well what they
are!"

The "rub-a-dub, dub" of the Candlestick-maker
clan,
Is really too vulgar, you think, to repeat;
While the patacake rhyme that pertains to the
Baker man,
Is childish in action, and lacking in feet.

Say, then, shall we sing you the Song of a Six-
penny?
Of twenty-four blackbirds all baked in a pie?
You answer, though conjurers often have tricks
many,
They cannot make blackbirds sing *after* they
die!

The "Cat and the Fiddle" you class as "chi-
merical,"
Like the dish that eloped with the spoon, as is
said,
You smile at the Ladybird's terror hysterical,
"Scarabæ Maculata," *you* call her instead.

You blame Mrs. Spider for hastening to vivisect
The fly who her parlour had sought to explore;
And as to the mansion where Jack was the
architect,
Too much iteration you think is a bore!

If you hear the sad story of Rock-a-bye baby too,
That "Gravity's laws," you remark, are in-
fringed,
And as to Miss Muffett, you call her a Gaby too,
And even opine that her mind was unhinged!

Ah! child of the century! Life goes too rapidly,
What with High Schools, and Board Schools,
and "Standards" unknown,
No wonder the old Nursery Rhymes echo vapidly
In brains half exhausted ere yet they are
grown!

"SWEET SEVENTEEN"

OH sweet Seventeen in the days that are perished,
How rosy her blushes, how modest her mien!
Guileless and good the illusions she cherished,
Childish perhaps, but still "sweet" seventeen.
To her, every dance was excitement unending,
She loved a new frock, and a raspberry tart;
To her, every partner seemed so condescending,
And each pretty speech as a truth from the heart!

But sweet Seventeen in the days now upon us,
Soars far beyond partners, and flounces, and jam,
She talks of her "views," she is reading for honours,
To pass in the Oxford or Cambridge Exam.
Her elders are snubbed, their opinions derided,
As "poor dear old fossils," and long left behind,
While with tresses cut short, and with garments divided,
Her *pince-nez* adjusted, she speaks out her mind!

Ah, sweet Seventeen, in those days unenlightened,
Could darn a silk stocking, or play a gavotte,
She read fairy tales, at hobgoblins was frightened,
And drew her romance from the pages of Scott.
Sentimental she might be, and ignorant rather,
She romped with the children, she rode like a bird,
But at least she loved home, and she honoured her father,
And ne'er even dreamed of disputing his word.

But sweet Seventeen in these days fast advancing,
She studies in science, and dabbles in doubt,
Has ideas upon Buddha, finds Balzac entrancing,
And argues Life's problems in season and out.
She cycles and smokes, and ignoring tradition,
She deems herself equal, or better than man;
In place of home duties, she seeks out a "mission,"
And scorns the old pathways wherever she can!

Ah, sweet Seventeen, in those past days lamented,
"To be a good girl" was the chief end she knew,
And I know not, if (*pace* these new lights invented)
This old aim is not the conclusion most true.

"All knowledge is gain," says the proverb of progress,
Those past days, perhaps, *were* a thought incomplete,
But in drawing the line 'twixt a fool and an ogress,
Beware, Seventeen, lest you forfeit the "sweet"!

"OUR country cousins!" Yes, they dwell
Far down among the Western Counties,
In that green West whose misty spell
Makes Nature lavish of her bounties.
Unknown in town,—they simply hail
From just a line of landed gentry,
And Fashion's World would surely fail
To know our cousins in the country!

These country cousins never tried
A Cambridge High Examination;
In fact, it cannot be denied
Theirs was a homely education!
But yet they seem to understand
All household things, from soup to sewing,
And deftly bring a willing hand
In hospitable care bestowing.

They know the poor about their gate,
Although they never heard of "slumming,"—
And round their father's small estate
All faces brighten at their coming!

The village choir their voices lead,
  They teach the village school on Sunday,
And in their secret souls we read
  A lurking awe of Mrs. Grundy!

For them no simple pleasures pall,
  They love their garden, dogs and ponies;
From parish feast to county ball,
  "*Ennui*" to them a thing unknown is.
So fair of face, of foot so fleet,
  Loving and loved, with hearts unclouded,
Our country cousins fresh and sweet
  Their happy lives by care unshrouded.

They follow in the good old ways,
  With small amount of worldly leaven,
And the "New Woman's" reckless craze
  Is all unknown to *them*, thank Heaven!
Aye, and we know it still holds true,
  That not in *one* such home, but dozens,
The length and breadth of England through
  We find their like—"Our Country Cousins!"

"A VALENTINE"

Past and Present

AH! the ironies of Fate!
Here's a note from you,—
February fourteenth, the date,
"Come and dine, now do!"

* * * *

Once upon a time, old friend,
Once upon a time!
You a different missive penned,
Clothed in halting rhyme!

Lace-edged note of dainty hue,
True-love knots galore,
Wreathed with blooms that never grew
In Dame Nature's store!

"Fair as rose, or lily white,
Is my Valentine,
Sweet as pink or pansy bright,
Rare as columbine!"

Thus and thus, the verses went,
  Then, a heart aflame,
Cupid with his bow well bent
  Taking deadly aim.

Crude enough! yet at the sight
  What a thrill was mine,
As I read with shy delight
  "To my Valentine!"

Now, St. Valentine's high Feast,
  Brings no answering joy,
No excitement in the least,—
  Goes without annoy.

Business letters, household bills,
  Notes and circulars,
Cause me no unwonted thrills,
  Leave no mental scars!

Once upon a time, old friend,
  Once upon a time,
This same writing you have penned
  Set my heart achime!

Now I read with tranquil nerve,
  "Will you come and dine?"
This, for middle age must serve
  As "a Valentine"!

THEN AND NOW

I. Retrospect

IT was somewhere in the sixties ere I took my
first degree,
Love's young dream one golden summer glorified
my life to be,
Present, past, and future blended in one fair, em-
bodied SHE!

Yes! her name was Henrietta, and she was but
seventeen,
And she wore a figured muslin, an enormous
crinoline,
While a chignon like a quartern loaf behind her
head was seen.

And many a happy visit to her Vicarage home
I paid,
And many a game of croquet on the level lawn
we played,
When she stamped her foot and scolded at the
blunders that I made!

I suppose she *had* a temper, but I liked her
cheeks aflame,
As her blue eyes flashed like needles when I
missed an easy aim,—
For she always came to help me at the finish of
the game!

Then our rambles in the moonlight, and our talks
beneath the trees,
Though I must confess she always was a most
determined tease;
The way she pinched my fingers, when I tried
her hand to squeeze!

Ah, that summer in the sixties! but it passed as
summers will,
And we drifted far asunder,—yet through years of
good or ill,
To revisit Henrietta has remained my purpose
still!

II. Reality

It was somewhere in the nineties, I had just been
made Q.C.,
And the light of love's young dream had paled
and left me fancy free,
For a robe and wig judicial was the dream most
dear to me!

It was on one fatal evening at a crowded London rout,
That a lady claimed acquaintance, she was rubicund and stout,
But I knew her not from Adam, though you seldom catch *me* out.

Then she shook a fat forefinger, asked me "how I could forget?"
She "would know me in a thousand, though 'twas years since last we met."
And her keen eyes flashed like needles;—O ye gods! 'twas Henriette!

"Distance lendeth," saith the proverb, "some enchantment to the view,"
Twenty years ago I never thought it could apply to *you*,—
O! my first love, Henrietta! yet the pity 'tis, 'tis true!

So we talked in friendly fashion o'er the days of long ago,
While I, musing, wondered vaguely what it was had changed her so,
Till I winced in sudden anger, as she said, "How bald you grow!"

Came a little man whose aspect was a chronic
state of scare,
"Don't you think, my love," he faltered, "that
the carriage must be there?"
Sternly Henrietta eyed him,—"Here's my husband, I declare!"

Once that *she* should have a husband would have
caused me poignant grief,
(Yet the changes Time can bring us sometimes
seem beyond belief),
Now that little man's existence is a most distinct
relief!

Ah! the rosy dreams of boyhood, how their
sunny memories thrill!
To revisit lost delusions proves sometimes a
bitter pill,—
So I wish that "Henrietta" had remained a
"memory" still!

Romance

"THE sea, the sea, the open sea!
The blue, the fresh, the ever free!"
How famed in song and story!
When the red sunset in the West
Calms down the wild white horses' crest,
And lulls the great sea into rest,
And sleep-enchanted glory.

For sound,—the rush of waters wide,
The lap and ripple of the tide,
Or roar of foaming breakers,—
The sea-birds' cry upon the gale,
The wind that pipes in shroud and sail,
Or comes and goes in fitful wail
O'er wastes of watery acres.

Or, sight more fair—smooth seas of light,
Green deeps between,—sun-sparkles bright,
  In silvery distance paling,—
That where the dim horizon lies
In misty blue would seem to rise,
And mingle with the far blue skies,
  Where dappled clouds are sailing.

The sea, the sea, how fair it shows!
Majestic in its vast repose,
  In song and story vaunted.
In calm and storm, in blue or grey,
In summer sun or winter spray,
For ever changing night or day,
  For ever mystery-haunted!

Reality

"The sea, the sea, the open sea!
And I am where I would not be!"
  Upon mid-ocean rocking.
Careless of life, in limp despair,
On cabin sofa hard and bare,
Where everything assumes an air
  Of misery and mocking!

For sound,—a trampling overhead,
Hoarse shouts, and heaving of the lead,
  The winds and waters warring;
Then dull vibrations throbbing through,
A pause, a quiver,—then anew,
The throbbing of that fiendish screw
  Through every fibre jarring.

For sight,—the low roof swaying slow,
The dull lamp swinging to and fro,
  In ceaseless, see-saw motion.
And worse,—beyond the narrow port,
Green, giddy waves, which sway and snort,
And heave, and sway again—in short,
  The see-saw of the ocean!

Then comes the stewardess with a grin,—
"Another hour, and we are in!"
  "An hour,"—of tribulation!
Ah, well, the sea's a subject wide,
Though glorious is the foaming tide,
It has for some a sadder side
  Of deep humiliation!

A CAPTIVE

A CAPTIVE! In whom hope is dead,
  Upon the stones he lies,
And dumbly droops his royal head
  With sad and sombre eyes.

A dingy roof shuts out the sky,
  And iron bars the light;
The weary day drags lagging by
  To weary, woeful night.

Ah! who may tell what visions gleam
  Before his silent gaze,
And pass in half-forgotten dream
  Of mirage-seeming haze!

He sees the tropic sunlight glare,
  Along the burning sand,
Where thorny scrub, and desert bare
  For countless miles expand.

He sees the forest dense and dim,
  The steaming swamp and pool,—
All trod by beasts its miry rim,
  As fain their thirst to cool.

He hears the roar that wakes the night,
  The doom of weaker prey:
The sullen stir of fret and fight
  Before the hush of day.

He sees them all, or foe or friend,
  In dreams the slow hours through;
And wakes, a Captive safely penned—
  A Lion at the Zoo!

CUPID IN THE GARDEN

As through her green garden a fair maid
went,
With never a whisper of danger nigh,
Who but Dan Cupid his way there bent,
For "love in idleness" grew thereby.

Gillyflowers, roses, and bergamot,
Bloom they bravely, but blooms she best,
Red picotee for a gay breast-knot,
To crown the posy she makes her quest.

"Hither, sweet boy, with the silver bow!
What doest thou in my garden glade?"
"Small is the boon I would crave, I trow,
'Tis but a posy from thee, dear maid!"

Roses she plucked for him, Love's own hue,
Nor recked the thorns that her fingers gall;
"Love lies bleeding," and lavender true,
And of her heartsease she gave him all!

Dan Cupid laughed as her lips he kissed,
  And slily fitting a shining dart,
That silver arrow that never has missed,
  Sent it straight to the fair maid's heart.

"Farewell!" he said; "I must needs be gone."
  "Hast thou never a posy for me?" she sighed.
"Go get thee a bough of the willow wan,
  And I will find thee the rest!" he cried.

* * * *

All in her green garden, ah, well-a-day!
  Mourns the poor maid in her misery;
For the sad-hued willow she wears to-day,
  With rue, and the woeful rosemary!

LOVE'S POSY

THROUGH twenty years doth Love his empire hold,
Deep in my heart from rosy spring to prime;
Too deep, is he? or I so little bold
That love so great should dwell there thus controlled
With dumb desire that lacks the wit to climb,
Through twenty years?

Nay, now for Love this posy sweet shall sue,
This love yet young, albeit the days are old,—
Blue lavender for truth, as I am true,
And passion-flushed carnation, Love's own hue,
And rosemary for memory's links of gold,
Through twenty years!

Through twenty years adown the slope of Time
My love has grown as once this posy grew,
Wear it, sweetheart! and learn from this poor rhyme
To crown at last with utmost bliss sublime
The heart which lived and loved and longed for you
Through twenty years!

ON THE BÜRGENSTOCK

August, 1891

THE wide blue arch of August noonday glowing
In blaze of sunshine as we climbed the hill,
With not a breath of faintest breeze soft blowing
So hushed it was, and still.

No sound to break the golden calm upheaving
Save the low hum of insects to and fro,
And far-off beat of steamer paddles cleaving
Lucerne's blue lake below.

White-starred Parnassus grass grows straight and slender,
With quivering harebells that reflect the sky,
While pink rest-harrow, and small eyebright tender
Along the pathway lie.

On the green summit where steep rocks hang over,
In giddy poise above the tranquil lake,
Rare butterflies on wings emblazoned hover
And airy pastime make.

Far off, through clear, transparent air thyme-laden,
In silver line the distant mountains rise;
The gleaming fairness of the white Snow Maiden
Kissed by the radiant skies.

And nearer yet, the play of sunlit shadows
On rolling hills and pine woods darkly green,
Where châlets cluster in the smiling meadows,
In summer peace serene.

And still, 'neath cloudy skies the thought we treasure
Of steep ascent, green pines, and towering rock,
That golden August day of charmèd leisure
Upon the Bürgenstock!

THE GLEN

SO fair the place! So green and peaceful seeming,
Green with the verdure of an older day,
Where Time's soft footstep stayed as if in dreaming
Upon his silent way.

There silvery boles of beeches rise majestic,
Like giants which some grove Primæval bore,
Carved with old names and letterings fantastic,
Which tell of days no more.

Chestnut and ash, and limes, their fragrance blending,
With breath of pines that steals upon the sense,
And great Scotch firs, their ruddy trunks ascending,
From laurel thickets dense.

So still it is,—save where with scant resistance,
The branches whisper in the Summer breeze,
And wood doves coo with fitful faint persistence,
Among the spreading trees.

So green the place! Save where the boughs
    retarding,
  Give glimpse of hill, and lock, and distant fen,
As if the ancient trees were joined in guarding
  The spell of that green Glen!

DRENAGH, *August*, 1897

OF THE DAYS OF OLD

Ballads

THE NORSEMAN'S FEAST

O THE storm wind howls
Where the grey wolf prowls,
By the ice on the frozen mere:
And the snow piled light
Hides the earth from sight,
Like a maid in white
On her bier.

But the cold bites not,
And frost is forgot
In hall, where the pine logs roar,
And the glow of the hearth,
Shines red through the garth,
O'er the snow-swept path
To the door.

In the murk and mist,
Do the wolves keep tryst,
Where the snow lies white on the wold.
But in torch-lit hall,
'Mid the shout of "Skäll!"
Recks nor jarl, nor thrall
Of the cold!

There the mead brims high,
And ere horns are dry
Does a toast echo brave and brief;
And the rafters ring,
As the old rhymes swing,—
"Skäll! skäll we bring
To the Chief!"

SONG

"Skäll! to the Viking!
Folk-ruler, war leader,
Strong arm for swift striking,
Wise wit for folk-pleader.

Skäll! to the fighter;
The Chief, fame achieving,
Skäll! to brain-biter!
His good sword skull-cleaving.

Skäll! to the Viking!
Strong hand on the war-bow,
Skäll! to him striking
The bears on the ice-floe!

Skäll! to him steering
To fight, his war-galley!
While against him anearing
No foeman dare rally.

Skäll! to the Viking!
  The toast that we swallow,
For love and for liking,
  To fare and to follow!"

. . . .

So the song is sped,
And the torches red
  Flame aglow in a fiery sheaf;
And again and about,
Does the toast ring out,
"Skäll! skäll," is the shout,
  "To the Chief!"

Subject given, "A TOAST."

THE VIKING'S GALLEY*

FROM the North Seas and the storm wind, from the wild Norwegian shore,
Comes an echo of the old time lost and gone for evermore;
Where the wash of waters soundeth, where the salt sea breezes blow
O'er the pinewoods stretching inland, o'er the ice field and the floe:
Hard by Tönsberg northern township, where the Viking's mound is made,
From those brave days long departed, comes a whisper from the shade;

* In a green mound, called King's Hill, near the Christiania Fjord, was discovered the perfect galley of a Viking, furnished with oars, mast, etc. Bones and remains of arms and treasure were in her hold, her free-board was hung with shields, and the skeletons of horses and hounds were buried near her. Seventy-three feet in length, the ship is evidently the tomb of a great chieftain, the idea of the ancients being, that at the last day the Vikings should be found ready equipped for battle, at the call of Odin. The rudder is also in position on the steer-bord in contradistinction to the leer- or empty-bord.

Like the gleam of dying beacon on the ancient
hills restored,
Comes the story of the death-ship by the Christiania Fjord.

There, beneath her mound sepulchral in the green
and level lea,
Lies the galley of the Viking, with her prow
towards the sea,
With the shields along her gunwhale, with her
mainsail ready rolled,
With her long oars laid amidships, and the treasure in her hold;
There the leader of the Norsemen in a fitting
tomb they laid,
Where the North Seas sound a *requiem*, and his
dirge the North wind made.

Ah! it may be o'er the North Seas, in the old
time long ago,
Proudly swept that warlike galley, bearing down
upon the foe;
While the long oars cleft the ocean and the fair-haired Norsemen shout,
As the war ships close together and the battle-cry rings out.
And the Viking led the onslaught, as among
the spears he stood,

While the fight waxed fierce and fiercer, and the
 decks ran red with blood ;
Ah ! it may be fighting bravely that he felt, or
 soon or late,
How the dark-veiled Norns mysterious held the
 threads of Death and Fate,
And that while he called on Odin, Victory-giver,
 God of War,
That he deemed the Valkyrs hovered on their
 white cloud steeds afar ;
Till the dread Wish-maids drew nearer, on his
 brow he felt their kiss,
Felt the solemn kiss that raised him out of battle
 into bliss :
And they bore his soul to Asgard, to Valhalla of
 the blest,
To the golden halls of Gladsheim, where the hero
 spirits rest.

But the dust of buried ages veils those ancient
 mysteries,
And the story of the Viking in the death ship
 hidden is ;
But we know they left him waiting with his
 horse and hound beside,
Waiting till the great All-Father, at the turning
 of the tide,

Calls him at the last awakening, when, in that dread battle day,
He shall rise and steer his galley from her moorings to the fray;
All equipped in shining armour, from the spirit land restored,
Steer her out into the North Seas from the Christiania Fjord!

"THE NORSE SHIPS AT NARBONNE" *

BALLAD

IT was the Emperor Charlemagne who feasted
all his host,
At Narbonne in the old time upon the southern
coast.
And at the royal palace and all the courts therein,
There was revel fair and stately, of peer and
paladin;
When lo! unto the harbour sailed in before the
breeze,
Up to the walls of Narbonne long ships from
over seas.

* Charlemagne was at the town of Narbonne on the Mediterranean, when some strange galleys appeared in the harbour. Some pronounced them Jewish or African traders, but the Emperor saw at once they were Norse sea rovers, and commanded they should be attacked and driven off. He watched their departure from the window with tears, and then turning to his wondering nobles, he said, "Savez-vous, mes fidèles, pourquoi je pleure amèrement? certes je ne crains pas que ces pirates me nuisent, mais je m'afflige profondément de ce que, *moi vivant*, ils ont été près de toucher ce rivage, et je suis tourmenté d'une douleur violente, quand je prévois tout ce qu'ils feront de maux à mes neveux et à leurs peuples."—*Histoire de France.*

Before the Emperor Charlemagne straightway
they brought the news,
Some thought them Moorish merchants, deemed
some that they were Jews;
But Charlemagne eyed them fiercely, and swore a
solemn oath,
"These are no honest traders, but thieves and
pirates both!
Go! man our swift war galleys, and smite them
to their knees,
These Vikings from the North land, who dare
come over seas."

It was the Emperor Charlemagne, who, 'mid
his peers that night,
Looked round him heavy hearted, on Warriors
proved in fight,
On Roland proud and peerless, on Oliver the
brave,
On Baldwin, Reynold, Turpin, Gerhardt, and
Alcuin grave,—
In Narbonne's ancient city, a goodly company,
With Ogier the Dane's-man, who came from over
sea.

Rose up the Emperor Charlemagne, gazed from
the window far,
And saw the Norsemen's long ships sail out beyond the bar!

They spread their brown sails seaward, a grim
defiance throw,
Then fast toward mid ocean, they flee before the
foe:
And Charlemagne watched their galleys, with
anguish and ill-ease,
From Narbonne's ancient city, sail onward over
seas.

It is the Emperor Charlemagne who to his Nobles
speaks,
"My lieges, do ye marvel that tears are on my
cheeks?
That I, whose realm extendeth till half the world
is mine,
From Ebro to the Danube, from Loire unto the
Rhine,
Burgundia, Spain, and Allemaine, with Rome and
Lombardy:
That I should weep when Norsemen sail here
from over sea?

"Nay!" spake the Emperor Charlemagne, "it is
not this I weep,
These Norse thieves dare no doing whilst I the
sceptre keep!

But in the darkling far-time, when I am cold and dead,
My soul misgives me sorely, with bodings dim and dread;
When I, entombed at Aächen, my sword across my knees,
Sleep sound, nor heed the storm cloud that gathers over seas.

When I, the Emperor Charlemagne, I robed and crowned alone,*
In Aächen's vaulted cloister sit dead upon my throne,
From over seas, I know it, shall fierce Norse hordes aspire
To vex my land and kinsmen, with track of blood and fire;
And if to Narbonne's city, they steer in days like these,
So woe to France hereafter, shall come from over seas!"

* Charlemagne, as is well known, was entombed sitting upright upon his throne—with his crown and robes and his sword "joyeuse"—in the vaults at Aachen (Aix-la-Chapelle).

Subject given, "OVER-SEAS."

Part I

WITHIN the walls of Leyden, a desperate people wait,
Despair, and pest, and famine wax sore within the gate.
From hot July till August, 'neath suns that mocked like flame,
All through that awful summer, till black September came.

The Spaniards from Vlaardingen pressed closer day by day,
(At Delft the troops of Orange, too far for succour lay;)
They cut the dyke at Schiedam, and let the sluices through,
"A drowned land, than a lost land, were better of the two!"

But the winds of heaven were silent, at ebb the
still tide slept,
And though the dykes were open, slow, slow the
waters crept,
And still the siege grew straiter, and direr was
the need,
And Valdez bade, "Surrender! Your lives shall
be the meed!"

"Nay, death before dishonour!" the starving
people cried,
"We wait till ships of Orange sail up the rising
tide."
From Rotterdam to Schiedam, from Delft unto
the sea,
They knew the dykes were open, yet ne'er a ship
there be.

"Up! up the Tower of Hengist! look o'er the
flood afar,
Ho, burghers, watch the coast line, if near the
white sails are."
They climb the Tower of Hengist, above the city's
height,—
Wide lay the shining waters, but ne'er a sail in
sight!

Woe, woe was there in Leyden, the famine fang
 struck deep,
And strong men dropped plague-stricken, and
 children died like sheep.
The Spanish swords pressed nearer, the Spanish
 fire waxed hot,
Yet keener was the anguish for the children that
 were not.

They climb the tower of Hengist, they look or
 far or wide,
But the winds of heaven were silent, and shallow
 lay the tide.
Then mad, the people clamoured to noble Vander
 Werff,—
"Give up the town, 'twere better to live as slave
 and serf!"

Outspake the Burgomaster, "Nay, slay me an ye
 will,
So help me, God, while living, I'll hold the city
 still;
Yea! ere the accursed Spaniard the outer gate
 should win,
I would fire the town of Leyden, and the gallant
 hearts within!"

It fell in mid September, the fleet set sail at last
With eight hundred men of Zealand, who served
before the mast.
They anchored at Land Scheiding, five miles from
Leyden town,
But the tide would serve no further, and the sea
was going down.

And Valdez taunted fiercely, "As well your
Prince may try
To sail his ships to Leyden, as stars from out
the sky!"
While still in grim defiance, the men of Leyden
wait
The black death looming near them, the ships
that tarry late.

But with dawn of grey October the darkest hour
was o'er,
The patriot prayers were answered, in the Heaven-
sent tempest's roar.
For through the night till morning there blew
the winds of God,
Until the dykes were flooded, the sea swept o'er
the sod.

From Leyderdorp to Lammen, the troops of Spain
kept guard,
Till deep seas surged around them, and foemen's
steel pressed hard.
Then fiercely raged the battle, and thickly fell
the slain,
That night, when sea and swordcraft broke down
the power of Spain.

Once more the men of Leyden, heartsick with
long delay,
Climbed up the Tower of Hengist when dawn
broke dim and grey;
Then o'er the waste of waters uprose a mighty
cry,
As to the walls of Leyden, the ships came sweep-
ing by!

Part II

"A rescue! ho, a rescue!" the famished Burghers
cried,
"For lo, the ships of Orange sail up the rising
tide;
Up, up, ye men of Leyden! Thank God on bended
knee,
In direst need a rescue He sendeth from the
sea!"

Then from half-ruined houses, all scarred by shot
and ball,
And down the grass-grown streetways, and on
the battered wall,
Went all the city seaward—all there were left to
go,
Left by the siege and famine, left by the Spanish
foe.

Men came there gaunt and haggard, and women
wan and weak,
That grey October morning, with pinched and
pain-drawn cheek;
And all along the quay-side a deathlike calm
they keep
Till up the great canal stream they see the long
oars sweep.

Then rose a shout of welcome, from every heart
aglow,
'Mid sighs and broken murmurs the crowd surged
to and fro;
And fast, from poop and porthole, the sailors
bring their store,
As to the starving people they fling the food
ashore.

* * * *

There wound a long procession through Leyden
streets that day,
Led by the Burgomaster, and marshalled on its
way.
Knights, soldiers, sailors, townsmen, with wives
and children went,
In endless stream slow moving, as if with one
consent.

Up to the old Cathedral they pass with one
accord,
That there, they may in worship give thanks
unto the LORD;
There in one vast *Te Deum* a thousand voices
rise,
Till from full hearts o'erflowing, in sobs the
music dies.

Thus is the old brave story of Leyden's rescue
told,
And still the siege of Leyden is writ in words
of gold.

EL DORADO

IN the old brave days of our England's fame,
  In the old brave days of sword and song,
When her ships were handled by knights of name,
  And good Queen Bess held the sceptre strong.

Aye, in those brave days now so fair, so far,
  In Bideford Town was stir and shout,
When down Torridge tide and across the bar,
  Came ships for the West a-sailing out.

It was Westward Ho! with the Devon men,
  Their white sails set to the freshening breeze,
And many and many a summer then
  They sailed in hope to the Indian seas.

And many a gallant, his heart aflame,
  Sang "Westward Ho!" in those old brave days,
Afire for the vision that never came,
  For "El Dorado," the golden maze!

And under the lee of the blue Azores,
  They sailed with the land breeze in their wake,
And along the palm-crowned Barbados' shores,
  By the mangrove swamps and rank cane brake.

Along, and along 'neath the tropic skies,
  And strange, rich life of the tropic seas;
The wealth of the Indies before their eyes,
  In gorgeous Isles of the Caribees.

The lust of plunder, the fever of fight,
  It bore them West, to the Spanish Main,
And whenever a Spanish sail they sight,
  No quarter then for "the dogs of Spain!"

But the Spanish swords were sharp and keen,
  Ere the flags were struck their decks ran red;
And pestilence lurked in the dense, damp green,
  Of fern-clad forests so fair bespread.

And so year by year as the ships came back,
  Back from the West with their spoils weighed
    down;
There were few to come, and many that lack
  Of men who sailed from Bideford Town.

But still that vision that never they found,
  Gleamed like a mirage their hearts to hold,
For somewhere they knew, in enchanted ground,
  Lay "El Dorado," the Land of Gold!

ELIZABETH'S GARDEN AT HEIDELBERG

FROM the old past a shadow falls—
  O'er Heidelberg it lingereth—
Of the old lives in those old walls,
From days long dead an echo calls,
  So faint and far—"Elizabeth!"

The glory is departed now,
  From barbican and battlement;
And high o'er Neckar's tranquil flow,
Red ruin and Time's vengeance slow
  On Heidelberg is evident.

The English palace silent stands,
  'Mid desolation desolate,
Which Frederick raised with loving hands
For her, who came to sway the lands
  Of all the fair Palatinate.

Those courts that stately rose to greet
  The young Electress Palatine,
Are roofless now; yet at their feet
Her garden green is growing sweet,
  With roses pale and eglantine.

Still stands the ancient gateway there,
  Like some stone-carven monolith,
Where scrolls of quaint device declare
How Frederick made that garden fair
  For "his loved wife, Elizabeth."

And there, when through blue Summer days
  Slow dropped each silver rivulet,
She loved across the flowers to gaze,
Where forest depths and woodland ways
  Swept downwards from the parapet.

So long ago! and then there came
  A day of fateful pageantry,
When Frederick and his knights of fame,
One dim November rode to claim
  Bohemia's crown and sovereignty.

She left her garden's mossy sward,
  She left her Castle Palatine,
And followed to the field her lord,
Nor flinched the foemen's fire and sword,
  The risk of charge and countermine.

But to that home she loved so well
  Came nevermore Elizabeth,—
Discrowned, in exile year by year
She dwelt; while ever-boding fear
  Sad Heidelberg encompasseth.

For soon its glory low is laid,
  And those high Courts are desolate;
Fell war through thirty years has made
A haunted waste, a desert shade—
  Of the once fair Palatinate!

* * * *

Now over Heidelberg there stays
  A silence that continueth,
That holds dead names of those old days,
Of her who loved those garden ways,
  The Queen of Hearts, Elizabeth!

"THE TERROR BY NIGHT"

The Plague Year in London. 1665.

"The pestilence that walketh in darkness, . . . the sickness that destroyeth in the noonday."—PSALM xci. 6.

O DARK the shadow for ever looming
 Through sweltering days unto airless night!
Where the Pestilence walketh in darkness glooming,
 And the Terror standeth before our sight!

O pitiless sky! Like brass beyond us,
 The red sun scorching with poisoned breath;
O awful silence that waxeth round us,
 And the Terror that guardeth the gate of Death!

Is it days or years, since the town was flying?
 Since the Church was closed? for the priest lay cold,
His last prayers said over dead and dying
 Ere the Terror tightened its icy hold.

Where strong, sick odours from braziers burning,
  There is scarce a house lacks the seal of mourning,
That brand on the door where the Cross is set,
  Show the Terror hath entered which none may let.

Never a sound save the Death cart moving,
  The clang of the bell—"Bring out your dead!"
Save the wail despairing of lone and loving,
  Where the Terror enters with stealthy tread.

Never a footfall in streets deserted,
  Where the grass grows green in the paven way,
Where the crumbling gables turn half averted,
  From the Terror that walketh by night and day!

O awful shadow! no hope forthgiving,
  That broods for ever on that black year
When was quenched all love and light of living,
  And the Terror hovered so near, so near!

* * * *

But all things pass, and Life's pulses languish:
  Was it yesterday? or so long ago?
God keep us all from such time of anguish
  And the Terror that walketh the way of woe!

A MEMORY OF THE "'FORTY-FIVE"

AFTER long years of exile and attainder,
After long years of heaviness and woe;
Back in the twilight of Life's sad remainder,
In the old home I left so long ago.

Back, by the grace of Hanover's hard pardon,
Home to the dear blue hills of Aberdeen;
Where smoke-stained towers and desolated garden
Hold but the shadow of what once has been!

Home? Yet the ones who made it so are vanished,
Slain years ago, or exiled over seas;
Lands lying waste, and clansmen dead or banished,
Scotland's cup of sorrow drained unto the lees!

Dark rise the hills beyond the ruined village,
Floats the white mist across the tarn below,—
As in that home half wrecked by war and pillage,
I dwell 'mid ghosts who loved it long ago.

Oft in the gloaming, ere the day has parted,
They come before me, still as when alive,—
Husband and sons, who left me gallant-hearted,
Slain at Culloden in the 'Forty-five.

Widowed and childless,—oftentimes in danger,
Exiled my King, and all the land in chains,
His rightful throne usurped by foreign stranger;
Woe's me! what comfort here on earth remains?

* * * *

Nay, there is this! A Faith that wavered never,
True to the Cause, though beaten and betrayed;
Through life and death, a loyalty which ever
Upheld the honour of the White Cockade!

AT THE GALLEYS

FREEDOM? Free? What does it stand for?
Stinging stripes and burning brand, or
Clanking chains on foot or hand for keeping off the death I crave!
Free? the word is null and senseless, to my dull ears, and defenceless
I, accurst in soul and body as a slave!

In the galley's hold infernal, strain we at a toil diurnal,
Where the torture seems eternal, and no mortal power can save;
In that galley thrice accursèd, burns an anguish unrehearsèd,
As a foretaste of hell's torment for the slave!

Through the long night dim and dreary, when the very moon aweary
Shines with fitful gleam and eerie, as the corpse light of the grave;
Till the sad, unwished-for morning, brings new stripes, and sweat, and scorning,
Creak of oars, and clank of fetters for the slave.

While the living, laden galley ploughs and heaves
 along the valley,
Where the green seas sob and sally in the deep
 trough of each wave;
And the salt breeze sears and scorches, and the
 hot sun flames like torches
On the blistered brow and shoulders of the slave!

At the long oars with our fellows, till the day's
 heat wanes and mellows,
And the sunset glory yellows all the West in
 lustre brave;
But that glory little matters to a thousand men
 in fetters,
To the homeless, hopeless anguish of the slave.

THE BALLAD OF THE KING OF SPAIN'S DAUGHTER

PART I

IN the time gone by for ever,
  In the old time that we sing,
Came a vision sleep-enchanted
  To the daughter of the king:
To the King of Spain's fair daughter,
  In her deep sleep of the night,
And a hero stood before her,
  Wondrous in his grace and might.
And his nobleness and glory,
  Filled her heart with love profound,
Till she vowed to seek him ever
  If she sailed the whole world round.

Tarried not the king's fair daughter,
  Left her sunny land of Spain,
In a mighty galleon sailing
  O'er the white waves of the main.

And from harbour unto harbour,
  And to England's white-cliffed strand,—
To "the green Isle of the Ocean*
  At the end of all the land,"—
To the rocky shores of Erin,
  To the harbour of Lochlinn,—
And at every place she anchored,
  Every port she entered in,
There the nobles all were bidden,
  And high festival they held,
Shone the wine in cup and beaker,
  While the sweet harp music swelled.

Yet nor East nor West her dream-knight
  Could the king's fair daughter see,—
And amid the mirth and feasting
  Pale and sad alone was she.

Onward still the mighty galleon,
  Slowly moving evermore,—
Sailing through the waste of waters,
  Land-locked bay, or sandy shore,—
Past "the land beneath the Ocean,"†
  The flat Island of Tyree,—
Past the coast of Ardnamurchan,
  In the Hebridean Sea;

* Isle of Tyree. † Scandinavia.

Till the great ship steering northward
  Came at last upon a day,
Unto "Mull of the great mountains,"
  And to Tobermory Bay.

And again the guests were bidden,
  And the red wine flowed on board;
While the foremost of the chieftains,
  Came proud Duart's gallant lord.
Glad was then the royal maiden,
  Joyful grew her heart and fain,
For she knew her dream's fulfilment,
  And her love was not in vain.

Ah! the fateful hour of meeting!
  And the fatal spell that bound,
As the web of Fate is woven,
  And the death-clouds gather round.

But on board the lordly galleon,
  And to Tobermory Bay,
At the summons of the princess
  Came the chiefs in brave array;
And the heart of Spain's fair daughter
  Day by day more lightly beat,
All unwitting she of evil,
  Life and love to her were sweet.

And false Duart loved and lingered,
  And forgot all else beside,
And forgot the bride who waited
  In his castle by the tide.

* * * *

But the hand of vengeance stays not,
  And the weird must e'en be dreed,
When by treacherous doom o'ertaken
  Fire and darkness did their deed.
For nor hurricane, nor tempest,
  Made the mighty galleon reel,—
(As she lay at anchor riding,)—
  From her topmast to her keel!

Then, by Mull of the great mountains,
  Rose the dark waves into spray—
When the great ship, heeling over,
  Sank, with all who in her lay!

Woe then to the Lord of Duart,
  And a stricken man was he,—
As the pale dawn slowly breaking
  Shone on wreck and troubled sea;
O, and darkly frowned the chieftain,
  And in secret grief he sighed
When the sea gave up her burden,
  At the turning of the tide.

At his word the fair drowned maiden
  At the mirk hour of the night,
Did they bear in gloom and silence,
  To the kirkyard on the height;
Ne'er a bell was tolled in passing,—
  Ne'er a Benedictus said,
As they left her there unshriven,
  With a green turf at her head.

Part II

Years went by, till one dark midnight,
  In the old time far away,
Stood a watcher keeping vigil
  In the kirkyard by the bay:
When at midnight's hour of magic,
  In a dim procession slow,
Came the dead in shadowy presence,
  Passing ghostly to and fro.

But the awestruck mortal, trembling,
  Marked one white form all alone,
Ever in the darkness mourning
  With a low heart-broken moan.
Prayers to all the saints he muttered,
  And the holy sign he made,
Ere he spoke, in pity seeking
  How her spirit he might aid.

At his living voice of greeting,
  Straight the seal of Death is freed,
And the shade of Spain's sad daughter
  Spoke, and told him all her need.

Told him of her Spanish kindred,
  Of her state and high degree,—
Till that vision sleep enchanted
  Shone across the Western sea.
Told him how the dream-spell lured her
  O'er the salt seas day by day,—
Like the shooting star of midnight,
  Or the sky-fire's* fitful ray,—
How she sought her dream-knight ever,
  How she sailed from shore to shore,—
Till her star in death-clouds darkling
  Set in gloom for evermore.

"Even death," she moaned, "oh! stranger,
  To my soul no peace can bring,
In a grave unblessed, unhallowed—
  I,—the daughter of a king!
Ah! in Heaven's dear mercy aid me,
  Couldst thou wash my bones from stain,
In the sainted well of Lismore,
  Saint Molúag's holy fane;

* Lightning (*Gaelic*).

Then to rest in Spanish country,
  Couldst thou bear them o'er the sea,—
Rich my sire shall make thy guerdon,
  Store of good red gold and fee.
Holy Church might then absolve me,
  Masses for my soul be said,
And by holy rites commended,
  Laid among the quiet dead,
Peace at last from Heaven descending
  O'er my weary soul be shed."

Then he promised, sore misdoubting,
  But he followed all her will,—
Washed her bones in Lismore's fountain,
  Saint Molùag's holy rill;
And to Spain he bore them seawards—
  Journeying ever long and late,
Told before the king her father,
  All his hapless daughter's fate.

And the king gave royal guerdon,
  Of red gold and precious store;
But a vengeance all-consuming
  On her cruel foes he swore.

Then, the Princess' prayer fulfilling,
  Are her bones in quiet laid,—
Holy Church a sanction granting,
  In the cloister's hallowed shade—

Swells the chant of solemn anthem—
  Mass is said, and censers swing,
White-robed priests beside her kneeling
  Daily Misereres sing.

Peace at last from Heaven descending,
  Brings her restless shade release,—
Sleeps the King of Spain's fair daughter,
  Rests her weary soul in peace.*

* From an old Highland legend, related by Dr. Norman Macleod. The tomb of the "Spanish Princess" is still shown in the churchyard of Morva, in Mull. The ship is said by tradition to have been blown up by some of Duart's clansmen.

THE WILFUL PRINCESS;

Or, the Legend of King Grislybeard. (GRIMM.)

'TWAS "once on a time," as the children say,
When the world moved slowly and life was gay, and kings and knights came awooing,
There lived a young princess so wondrous fair,
That gallants in plenty came courting there,
But her blue eyes scorned as they laughed—"Beware!" to many a man's undoing.

They sued for her favour on bended knee,
But she threw back her pretty head in glee, unmoved by passion or pleading;
For "one is too stout, and the next too small,
That is too ugly, and this is too tall!"
She flouted and frowned at them one and all, no matter their birth and breeding!

At last came a suitor of royal race,
With a martial bearing, and stern, brave face,
though his hair was frosted lightly.
And her heart went out to him unaware,
Yet still must she mock at his stately air,—
"'King Grislybeard' is his name, I declare!" then
blushed, with a pang, contritely.

He went like the rest,—but the king her
sire,
Cried shame on the princess, and swore in ire,
"Thou hast need of sharper schooling!
And since thou hast scorned a good man
and true,
Be it beggar or prince, who next comes to
woo,
Thou shalt wed him straight without more ado,
and make an end of this fooling!

Full soon to the castle a beggar came,
Close hooded and bent, and ragged and lame, to
ask an alms in the gateway.
"Lo! here," said the king, "is thy bride-
groom, maid!"
And in vain the princess implored, and
prayed,
The word had gone forth that must be obeyed,
and the wedding was ordered straightway.

Oh! never was seen so woeful a bride,
As she and the beggar-man side by side, stood hand in hand at the altar!
With an iron grip did he hold her neared,
As if even then, to lose her he feared;
And "Alas!" she thought, "for King Grislybeard!" 'mid the tears that made her falter.

She was wed; they bade her in scorn, "good speed!"
As the beggar his royal bride would lead away to his distant dwelling.
Scant were his words, but both tender and strong
Was the arm that guided her steps along,
As if he were fain to soothe the wrong which had set her sore heart swelling.

"Tell me, I pray," said the princess at last,
"Whose the broad lands and the woods we have passed? and the castle so vast and splendid?"
"Fair wife, see as far as the eye can fall,
The man whom thou once in thy jest didst call
'King Grislybeard,' he is the lord of all; thou shalt go there for alms!" he ended.

"Nay, now! of thy pity, not there, I trow!"
In vain—as a beggar she needs must go,—her
will is swayed by a stronger.
"Who comes from the castle?" — "The
king!" they cried,—
"Here! take thy dole, maiden, and stand
aside——"
With her beggar lord was she fain to hide, but
lo! he was there no longer!

His cowl and crutch on the ground were
thrown,
And instead stood King Grislybeard alone, and
smiled as he towered above her;
"Oh, princess! thy pride it was hard to
beat,
But thou art worth all the winning, sweet!
My heart and crown will I lay at thy feet, so
thou take me for lord and lover."

Thus the wilful princess had found her lord,
Found the will that ruled, while the heart adored,
and her tears were turned to laughter.
So runs the old tale of a bygone day,
Of the times and peoples long passed away,
And the story ends, as the children say,—"They
lived happy ever after!"

THE LITTLE DANCING GHOST

BALLAD

IT was Christmas Eve, and the pale moon shone
  On the floor of the old oak hall,
While the logs blazed high on the open hearth
  And lit up the panelled wall.

And sitting idly beside the fire,
  I opened the quaint spinet,
Touching the keys with a careless hand,
  In a mood of vague regret.

The old walls echoed the tuneful notes
  As my fingers lightly strayed;
Till an old gavotte of long ago
  I softly and slowly played.

What is it floats from the shadows dim,
  Softly with never a word,—
Moving in time to the measured air,
  As the quaint old tune is heard?

What is it floats o'er the polished floor,
  Where the fire and moonlight meet?—
A spirit?—Ah! no, it was only this,
  Just a little pair of feet!

Only two little white dancing feet,
  Moving in time to the air;
Two little feet in their high-heeled shoes,
  That are tripping so lightly there.

So slowly the music comes and goes,
  With a sighing as of tears;
But the little white ghost that owned them
    once
  Has been dead for ninety years!

* * * *

It was long ago, the old story tells,
  On a snowy Christmas Eve,
That the squire's fair daughter left her home,
  Nor asked for her father's leave.

That Christmas Eve in the old oak hall,
  They held high festival there,—
And hers was the lightest foot of all,
  And hers was the face most fair.

Oh! blithely she danced the last gavotte,
  As the signal for their flight;
And then, with her lover by her side,
  Stole forth in the wintry night.

Out in the night, 'neath the frozen stars,
  Where the snow was lying deep;
And they must ride o'er the trackless wolds,
  For the road they may not keep.

There was mirth and song in the hall that night,
  And the old walls brightly glow;
But little they reck that the maiden fair
  Is lost in the cruel snow.

Lost in the snow on the pathless wolds,
  Where no human care can save;
And the Christmas joy-bells ring her dirge,
  And the snow-drifts make her grave.

*   *   *   *

But ever since upon Christmas Eve,
  When the snow and moonlight meet;
And we play the air of the old gavotte,
  Come the little dancing feet.

Poor little feet, in their high-heeled shoes,
  Whose treading no mortal hears;
From the shadowy snows and the spirit land,
  From the dust of ninety years! *

* Founded on a story in *All the Year Round*.

IN THE COURTS OF THE TEMPLE

"DEFENDERS OF THE FAITH"*

LONG ago, when men were wont to travel
  Those good ways wherein their fathers trod,
And no mysteries must needs unravel,
  Glad in simple faith to worship God—

Then it was, when folk in church assembled,
  As the bell for Matins sounded clear,
And on steel and brass the sunbeams trembled,
  That an ancient rite they counted dear.

Through the choir sweet echoes fade and falter,
  As the anthem's silver tones recede;
And the white-haired priest before God's altar
  Sounds the solemn cadence of the Creed.

* "In Poland and Lithuania the nobles used formerly to draw their swords when the Creed was recited, in token that, if need were, they would defend the Truth, and seal it with their blood."—*Wheatley.*

Instant, as the sacred words come slowly,
  Shining sabres from their scabbards clash;
Every man repeats the refrain holy,
  Every sword is lifted as one flash!

"I believe,"—in solemn voice sonorous,
  And with swelling tone the answer came,—
"I believe,"—in mighty growing chorus,
  "I believe in God's thrice Holy Name."

"I believe!" in sound that volume gathers,
  Thus in token vowed they to the Lord;
To uphold the Faith held by their fathers,
  Even to defend it with the sword!

Then for Holy Church the prayer succeeding,
  Every sword is sheathed with clank of steel;
"Militant on earth,"—their voices pleading,
  As "Defenders of the Faith" they kneel.

BEFORE THE ANGEL

"When thou goest into the house of GOD . . . suffer not thy mouth to cause thy flesh to sin, neither say thou before the angel . . ."—ECCLES. v. 1, 6.

THROUGH the whole great church there are
lights ablaze,
When the bells are chiming for Evensong;
And many are gathered for prayer and praise,
And many the moods in that motley throng.

But a Listener listens,—unseen, unsought,
Who can weigh the worth of the incense
brought.

The priest and his people together kneel,
In solemn confession their accents meet:
Is it souls that thrill? is it hearts that feel?
Or only the lips making counterfeit?

But a Listener listens,—so still, so near,
Unto whom are the minds of men made clear,

Then the organ swells in triumphant tone,
  And voices are blending in glad accord:
Ah! say, do they sing with the words alone?
  Is it "out of the heart" that they praise the
      LORD?

    But that Listener listens, and few, how few
    Of those musical notes unto *him* ring true!

Alas! for the wandering thoughts that hold,
  Of this world's folly or trouble or gain;
For the earthbound spirit, the fervour cold,
  E'en in those who to pray are fain.

    Yet the angel Listener rejoices then
    O'er but one true prayer from the sons of men.

A CHRISTIAN MARTYR

(After the picture by De la Roche)

SHINES the fair moon with dim, uncertain gleam,
From cloudy midnight skies,
Where the broad river's length of tranquil stream
In dusky shadow lies.

Calm seems the hour, half darkness and half light,
Yet there upon the shore
Stand those whose hearts were heavy on that night,
And wrung with anguish sore.

For, in mid-stream where the dark current flows,
Upborne upon its tide,
Floats one, whose brow the white moon's radiance shows,
Unearthly—glorified.

A maiden soul, so steadfast in the Faith,
  Death brought but healing balm;
She, whose young life should know nor scar, nor
      scaith,
  Has gained the martyr's palm!

And as afar those watchers vigil keep,
  Over their loved one's rest,
Calm as a child new-rocked she seems to sleep
  Upon the river's breast.

To their sad hearts, untimely seemed her fate,
  In Death's dark waters drowned;
But there was joy above at Heaven's gate,
  A martyr spirit crowned!

THE IDEAL LIFE

THE life of old!
In joyous years that were,
Far back it lies, and fair,
Half hid in mists of gold,
For all is sunlight there.
A story that is told,
The life of old.

The life to be!
When youth and hope are met,
Upon the threshold set
Of Love's sweet mystery.
Doubt knowing not, nor fret,
So glad beseems and free
The life to be.

The life that is—
A round of calm routine,
Shadow and sun between,
Dreams dreamt, hopes gone amiss.
Unwrung by anguish keen,
Uncrowned by highest bliss,
The life that is.

The Life beyond—
  Lo! all that made life sweet,
  Fulfilled, restored, complete,
In God's eternal bond.
  There, there alone shall meet
All earth's ideals fond,
    In Life beyond!

SONNET

"'Tis better to have loved and lost,
Than never to have loved at all."

OH, Love, the lord of life, the key to all
The mysteries which heaven and earth contain.
Sweet Love, which honey brings to life, and gall,
Its keenest joy, and its most bitter pain.
True Love, whose high ordeal perfect made
Brings back a gleam of Eden's paradise;
Till taught to know by Death's all-conquering blade,
The anguish, and the crown of sacrifice.
To love and lose, or never love to know,
The first were best, than love without delight.
True Love knows not of loss, in utmost woe,
'Tis but Death's wing has shadowed our dim sight.
Love cannot die! Outliving earth and time,
High heaven shall solve its mysteries sublime.

A HAUNTED HOUSE

"A HAUNTED house!" where death and desolation
Seem stamped on every gable grey and grim,
Where nameless terrors bring a chill sensation,
The shadow of a mystery dark and dim.

Where every footstep echoes weird and hollow
Through empty corridor and broken stair,
While every wandering wind there seems to follow
A wail from out the darkness of despair.

Nay! there are other houses not less haunted,
Though no dim terrors mar *their* aspect bright,
Where sunshine reigns, and every wish seems granted,
And yet there lurks a shadow out of sight.

For there, one room is empty, swept and garnished,
Sunny and still, and sorrowfully neat,
With little cots in whiteness all untarnished,
Where never comes the sound of little feet.

Unchecked, the sunbeams through the lattice
slanting,
Make long bright rays along the nursery floor.
Without, the hum of bees, and thrushes chanting;
Within, a silence broods for evermore.

And yet, sometimes when summer days are
gleaming,
And drowsy noon has hushed all outward
tread;
Some loving hearts will hear, as in dim dreaming,
The trot of toddling footsteps overhead.

The sound of childish trebles and clear laughter,
From little hearts that have for long been
still;
Will hear, but only to remember after
The little graves upon the churchyard hill.

But only to remember of their leaving,
Each after each, to play in Paradise;
Those precious ones who were, 'ere Death's be-
reaving,
The heart's desire of some once happy eyes.

Such is the story of some haunted houses,
Which brings no sense of terror or dismay;
In truth, a gentle haunting which but rouses
The tender memory of a bygone day.

"IF"

IF thou art mine,—
  Then life for me is fraught
  With love transcending thought,
For all of me is thine.
  No soul beside is aught
If thou art mine!

If thou be true,
  I'll let the world go by,
  And Time and change defy,
Though roses twine with rue;
  Content to live or die
If thou be true.

If thou rejoice,
  Then all the world's bedight
  With sunshine and delight;
The music of thy voice
  Makes every shadow bright,
If thou rejoice!

If thou art sad,—
  For thee I suffer smart,
  And bear my swelling heart
As in grief's vesture clad.
  Dearest to me thou art,
If thou art sad!

If thou shouldst die,—
  Ah, pray that God may take
  This heart, that it may break,
And in Death's slumber lie
  For thy belovèd sake
If thou shouldst die!

April, 1890.

" MISERRIMUS " *

DIM the cloister shade, and cold,
Fell the twilight vaporous
On a gravestone worn and old,
Where the crumbling legend told
Only this,—" Miserrimus."

Feet of long forgotten dead,
Through the years monotonous,
Wore the stone above thy head,
Never one who stayed their tread
By thy grave,—" Miserrimus."

Never tear upon thy stone,
Never garland odorous;
None to kneel and pray alone
Where thou liest all unknown,
Thou, who wast,—" Miserrimus."

* In the North Cloister of Worcester Cathedral there is a gravestone on which is this sole inscription, " Miserrimus "—" Most miserable,"—and it has never been identified with any certainty.

Mourners bring their dead to lie
  In that cloister slumberous;
Carve their names and virtues high,
  Heedless that the tomb near by
    Only tells,—"Miserrimus."

Nay! a mystery profound
  Seals the silence tremulous;
Holds the piteous secret bound
  Of that woe that fettered round
    Thy sad soul,—"Miserrimus"!

Though no gleam in Time or space
  Pierce that veil mysterious;
Yet, God grant thou hast a place
  Where thou dwellest by His Grace,
    Never more,—"Miserrimus"!

Subject given, "A Mystery

THE WAY OF THE WORLD

"PRITHEE, Pilgrim, tell me true,
Whither wends this worldly way?
Whose the feet that tread it through,
What the landmarks lest they stray?"

"Stranger, lo! the way is old,
Short or lengthened, rough or smooth,
Man must wend it ere he wold,
For it must be trod, in sooth.

"Rosemary grows there, I wis,
Purple heartsease all unfurled,
And sad rue in plenty is
On this way of all the world."

"Pilgrim, say what perils are,
On this way where all must fare?"
"Thorns entangle, quagmires bar,
That unwary feet may snare.

"Divers pitfalls lurk therein,
  Satan spreads his lures apace,
Good and evil, grace and sin,
  Meet together face to face.

"Ragged beggars, sport of Fate,
  Queens in samite, crowned and curled,
Clown and noble, soon or late,
  Go this way of all the world."

"Pilgrim! sad meseems this way,
  If folk faint and fall thereon?"
"Nay, but let them strive and pray,
  Bravely fought is well nigh-won.

"Some there are who onward press,
  Plucking heartsease where they can;
Wear their rue with cheerfulness,
  With a strength not born of man.

"So they mount through toil and pain
  To the City gold and pearled,—
Steadfast souls do there attain,
  By this way of all the world!"

www.ingramcontent.com/pod-product-compliance
Lightning Source LLC
Chambersburg PA
CBHW020538270326
41927CB00006B/637
* 9 7 8 3 7 4 4 7 7 5 3 0 4 *